If you're reading our book, *Mingle*, then you're already a business networking Rockstar. Claim your FREE listing into the ONLY exclusive national business networking directory. Visit http://www.rockstarconnect.com.

MINGLE

The Art of Face-to-Face Networking in the Digital Era

Steven David Elliot and Nick Cioffi

An Actionable F2F Networking Journal

E-mail: info@thinkaha.com
20660 Stevens Creek Blvd., Suite 210
Cupertino, CA 95014

Copyright © 2018 Steven David Elliot and Nick Cioffi

All rights reserved. No part of this book shall be reproduced, stored in a retrieval system, or transmitted by any means other than through the AHAthat platform or with the same attribution shown in AHAthat without written permission from the publisher.

⇨ Please go to
http://aha.pub/Mingle to read this AHAbook and to share the individual AHAmessages that resonate with you.

Published by THiNKaha®
20660 Stevens Creek Blvd., Suite 210, Cupertino, CA 95014
http://thinkaha.com
E-mail: info@thinkaha.com

First Printing: November 2018
Hardcover ISBN: 978-1-61699-284-2   1-61699-284-0
Paperback ISBN: 978-1-61699-283-5   1-61699-283-2
eBook ISBN: 978-1-61699-282-8   1-61699-282-4
Place of Publication: Silicon Valley, California, USA
Paperback Library of Congress Number: 2018957201

Trademarks

All terms mentioned in this book that are known to be trademarks or service marks have been appropriately capitalized. Neither THiNKaha, nor any of its imprints, can attest to the accuracy of this information. Use of a term in this book should not be regarded as affecting the validity of any trademark or service mark.

Warning and Disclaimer

Every effort has been made to make this book as complete and as accurate as possible. The information provided is on an "as is" basis. The author(s), publisher, and their agents assume no responsibility for errors or omissions. Nor do they assume liability or responsibility to any person or entity with respect to any loss or damages arising from the use of information contained herein.

Acknowledgements

Special acknowledgements to Sarah Elliot and the Rockstar Connect team. Without them, there would be no Rockstar Connect and therefore, no book. Additional acknowledgement to Mitchell Levy of AHAthat for your stewardship in bringing this book to fruition.

Dedication

We dedicate this book to Sarah, Tian Yi, Stuart, Sharon, Eleanor, and Andrew, whom we love and respect with all our hearts.

How to Read a THiNKaha® Book

A Note from the Publisher

The AHAthat/THiNKaha series is the CliffsNotes of the 21st century. These books are contextual in nature. Although the actual words won't change, their meaning will every time you read one as your context will change. Be ready, you will experience your own AHA moments as you read the AHA messages™ in this book. They are designed to be stand-alone actionable messages that will help you think about a project you're working on, an event, a sales deal, a personal issue, etc. differently. As you read this book, please think about the following:

1. It should only take 15–20 minutes to read this book the first time out. When you're reading, write in the underlined area one to three action items that resonate with you.
2. Mark your calendar to re-read this book again in 30 days.
3. Repeat step #1 and mark one to three more AHA messages that resonate. They will most likely be different than the first time. BTW: this is also a great time to reflect on the AHAmessages that resonated with you during your last reading.

After reading a THiNKaha book, marking your AHA messages, re-reading it, and marking more AHA messages, you'll begin to see how these books contextually apply to you. AHAthat/THiNKaha books advocate for continuous, lifelong learning. They will help you transform your AHAs into actionable items with tangible results until you no longer have to say AHA to these moments—they'll become part of your daily practice as you continue to grow and learn.

Mitchell Levy, The AHA Guy at AHAthat
publisher@thinkaha.com

Contents

Section I
The Value of Physical Networking — 13

Section II
The Advantages of Hosting Your
Own Networking Event — 23

Section III
Strategies for Being Successful at
Physical Networking Events — 35

Section IV
Your Keys to Success in Building
a Good Referral Network — 55

Section V
Complement Your Physical Networking
with Social Media — 77

Section VI
Pitfalls of Networking to Avoid — 95

Contents

Section VII
Concluding Thoughts   103

About the Authors   113

Section I: The Value of Physical Networking

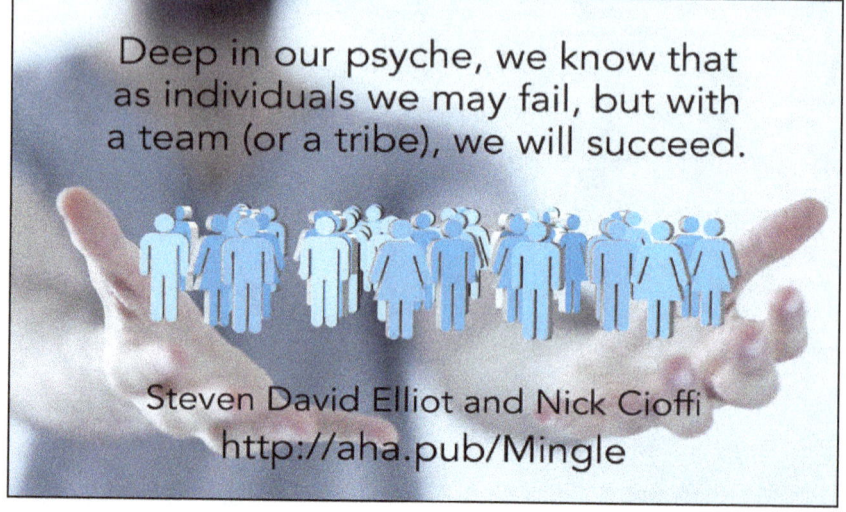

Share the AHA messages from this book socially by going to http://aha.pub/Mingle.

Section I

The Value of Physical Networking

Networking is a great way to meet people and build relationships. Without relationships, you don't have a business. The quality of the relationships you have is more important than the number of people you meet.

If done right, physical networking enables you to build authentic connections with other people. If you build meaningful connections through in-person networking, you're able to grow your sphere of influence, which can greatly help you reach your goals and succeed in business.

Section I: The Value of Physical Networking

1

Looking to network better and impress your online audience, read and share "MINGLE: The Art of Face-to-Face Networking in the Digital Era" at http://aha.pub/Mingle.
http://aha.pub/StevenDavidElliot
http://aha.pub/NickCioffi

_____
_____
_____

2

The more frequently you leave your cave and #Network, the more you're presented with a multitude of opportunities that will enhance your material and spiritual abundance.
http://aha.pub/StevenDavidElliot

3

Networking is like sales, where it's a numbers game; the more sales calls you make, the better. The more people you network with, the better. #NetworkMore
http://aha.pub/StevenDavidElliot

Section I: The Value of Physical Networking

4

Networking can be about self-actualization. If you want to be an altruistic and a benevolent person, do so at the networking events you attend.
http://aha.pub/StevenDavidElliot

5

Are you known in your local community? Physical networking is a great way for people to get to know you.
http://aha.pub/StevenDavidElliot

6

When you open the doors to new experiences through #Networking, you can create so many benefits not just to your business, but to the community as a whole. #BuildRelationships
http://aha.pub/StevenDavidElliot

_____

_____

_____

Section I: The Value of Physical Networking

7

Physical networking enables you to meet, interact, and get to know how other people act. That ability helps to make you a better leader, which is valuable for your business. http://aha.pub/NickCioffi

---

8

There's value in traditional networking (meeting people F2F) where you can be your authentic self. Are you being authentic? http://aha.pub/NickCioffi

---

9

The people you meet at networking events may not transact with you, but they have co-workers, friends, and family that could. Are you networking?
http://aha.pub/StevenDavidElliot

_____
_____
_____

10

At networking events, you get to expose yourself to people with different experiences from your own. By doing so, you become a more enlightened individual.
http://aha.pub/StevenDavidElliot

_____
_____
_____

Section I: The Value of Physical Networking

11

When you #Network with others, you must realize that they have different experiences from your own. This is a great opportunity to learn and grow. http://aha.pub/StevenDavidElliot

12

Whether it's learning about digital marketing or how to write a business check, the info you need can be obtained from your network. #Leverage http://aha.pub/StevenDavidElliot

13

When physical networking is done right, you are no longer just an individual; you're like a company of thousands of people—people who have your back and support you. http://aha.pub/StevenDavidElliot

_____

_____

_____

14

Deep in our psyche, we know that as individuals, we may fail, but with a team (or a tribe), we will succeed. http://aha.pub/StevenDavidElliot

_____

_____

_____

Section II: The Advantages of Hosting Your Own Networking Events

Share the AHA messages from this book socially by going to http://aha.pub/Mingle.

Section II

The Advantages of Hosting Your Own Networking Events

Attending networking events can bring you opportunities, but being the host of your own event significantly increases those opportunities. When you host a networking event, people want to get to know you. People attending events typically do their research to know who the host is and will go out of their way to meet them.

Hosting your own networking event enables you to make a name for yourself. You have a reason to play out your strengths and attributes on a bigger stage, which helps to demonstrate that you are an authority in what you do.

Section II: The Advantages of Hosting Your Own Networking Events

15

When you host your own networking event, you're making yourself the pretty girl at the dance or the big man on campus. Everybody will want to dance with you and get to know you better. http://aha.pub/StevenDavidElliot

16

By being a host of your event, everyone participating knows who you are—they typically know who the host is before they attend. #HostEvents
http://aha.pub/StevenDavidElliot

17

If you host your own networking event, you're someone who has proven your worth and you're accorded respect. #HostEvents
http://aha.pub/StevenDavidElliot

18

Hosting networking events can help you meet people who do exactly what you do as a career. It's where you can interact with them as friends and colleagues instead of competitors. #Leverage
http://aha.pub/StevenDavidElliot

19

At a networking event, you're with like-minded individuals who understand the path that you're on, and they're going to cheer you to your goal. You can't put a dollar value on that.
http://aha.pub/StevenDavidElliot

20

Hosting networking events helps you grow and improve. When you can interact with the greater community with more skill and efficacy, it's going to lead to more success in your business.
http://aha.pub/StevenDavidElliot

_____
_____
_____

Section II: The Advantages of Hosting Your Own Networking Events

21

Hosting an event gives you the opportunity to play on a big stage some of the attributes you may not do in your normal daily or career life. It's going to increase your self-esteem and morale, which will help you close more business.
http://aha.pub/StevenDavidElliot

22

When you actively network in person, your morale gets better and you become happier. It takes things that you can't experience through digital to truly #Connect with others.
http://aha.pub/StevenDavidElliot

23

If you host your own networking event, you have an excuse to talk to people about yourself and what you're doing. #HostEvents http://aha.pub/NickCioffi

24

If you host your own networking event, you have a reason to connect with people both in person and online, and welcome them to your network.
http://aha.pub/NickCioffi

25

If you host your own networking event, you have the ability to give something of value to people in person. #HostEvents http://aha.pub/NickCioffi

26

If you host your own networking event, you have a reason to reach out to people other than to sell them products. #HostEvents http://aha.pub/NickCioffi

27

When people see that you're sincere in helping them, you will garner trust and your name will be on their lips. They will see you as an expert at what you do, and they can become your brand evangelists.
http://aha.pub/StevenDavidElliot

28

If you host your own networking event, you have the ability to connect with people and allow them to contribute value to make them feel a part of your tribe. #GainingTrust http://aha.pub/NickCioffi

29

If you are well-known and lots of people like and trust you, you have an enormous advantage over competitors that are not known. #HostYourOwnEvent http://aha.pub/StevenDavidElliot

Section III: Strategies for Being Successful at Physical Networking Events

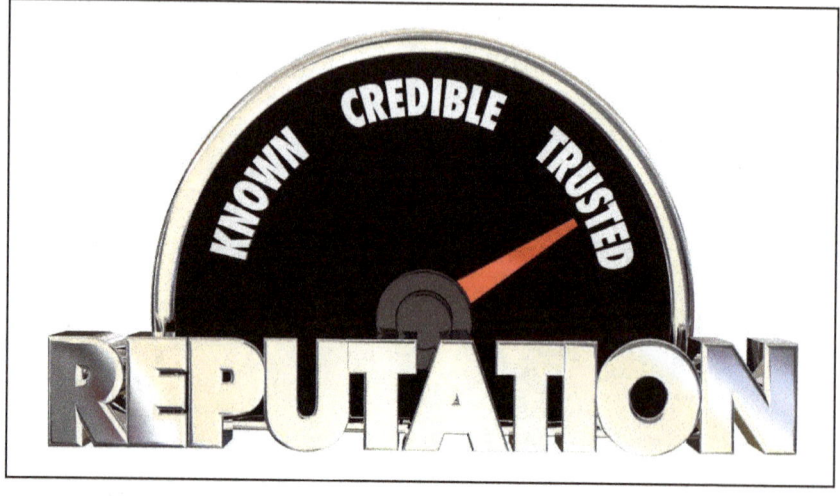

Share the AHA messages from this book socially by going to http://aha.pub/Mingle.

Section III

Strategies for Being Successful at Physical Networking Events

Physical networking events allow you to meet people who can potentially help you with your business. When physically networking, it's important to present yourself appropriately to gain people's respect and trust.

It's true that first impressions are significant. When you present yourself as someone worthy of being trusted, people will want to know and build a relationship with you. The way you dress and the way you behave in front of people will determine how people will look at and interact with you.

Section III: Strategies for Being Successful at Physical Networking Events

30

Whether it's in person or on social media, first impressions are very important. #NetworkingTricks http://aha.pub/NickCioffi

31

When you go to an event, your hair should be cut, your nails should be clean, and your clothing should show that you have pride in yourself. #NetworkingTricks http://aha.pub/NickCioffi

32

Follow the rules of etiquette. Don't interrupt other people's conversations, and don't interrupt the person whom you're speaking with. #NetworkingTricks http://aha.pub/NickCioffi

Section III: Strategies for Being Successful at Physical Networking Events

33

Don't go to networking events and trumpet the phenomenal things you've done. People will reject that and see you as a bragger. #BeHumble #NetworkingTricks http://aha.pub/StevenDavidElliot

34

Just because you have a microphone doesn't mean you should speak. It depends on who your audience is and whom you want to relate to. #NetworkingTricks http://aha.pub/StevenDavidElliot

35

When it's appropriate at networking events, you should expose your goals and aspirations. Some people are going to accept you warmly, while others are going to reject you. Learn from both extremes.
#NetworkingTricks
http://aha.pub/StevenDavidElliot

_____
_____
_____

Section III: Strategies for Being Successful at Physical Networking Events

36

Present yourself as someone who's interested in opportunities. How are you presenting yourself at events? #NetworkingTricks http://aha.pub/StevenDavidElliot

---

37

Your goal when you go to a networking event should be of #Cooperation or #Competition. How do you interact with other people? #NetworkingTricks http://aha.pub/StevenDavidElliot

38

When you go to a networking event and you feel that there's no one of value there, think again. If you made the proper impact, those people may help you formulate what you're actually trying to achieve. #NetworkingTricks
http://aha.pub/StevenDavidElliot

39

Physical networking is what we're naturally good at. If you put yourself out there for others to see, you're going to be rewarded tenfold. #NetworkingTricks
http://aha.pub/StevenDavidElliot

_____
_____
_____

40

When networking, think of how you can mesh your talent with other people so that you can accomplish things greater than the sum of its parts. http://aha.pub/StevenDavidElliot

---

41

After the networking event, have 1x1s with those with mutual interest in helping each other in the physical and social world. #NetworkingTricks http://aha.pub/StevenDavidElliot

Section III: Strategies for Being Successful at Physical Networking Events

42

When you go to a networking event, you will bring value to yourself by focusing on bringing value to others. #NetworkingTricks http://aha.pub/NickCioffi

43

A great networker is someone who goes to a networking event and sees it in an altruistic way and figures out how to help others. #NetworkingTricks http://aha.pub/NickCioffi

44

When going to networking events, always think of the other person and how you can help them before thinking of yourself. The people you help will reward you. #NetworkingTricks http://aha.pub/StevenDavidElliot

---

Section III: Strategies for Being Successful at Physical Networking Events

45

One key trick to being an effective networker is being a good listener. Ask people about what they're trying to achieve and what they've done. #NetworkingTricks
http://aha.pub/StevenDavidElliot

46

Ask other people what they're trying to achieve and how you can help them achieve it. This allows you to be seen as a giver, a helper, and an authority in whatever you choose to do. #NetworkingTricks
http://aha.pub/StevenDavidElliot

47

When you provide support for other people, there's a better chance that they will like you and want to get to know you better. Are you doing good things that will help people like you? #NetworkingTricks
http://aha.pub/StevenDavidElliot

_____

_____

_____

Section III: Strategies for Being Successful at Physical Networking Events

48

It won't matter how many people you meet at a networking event if you don't demonstrate that you're the type of person who will bring value to others. #NetworkingTricks
http://aha.pub/StevenDavidElliot

49

The best goal that you can have at a networking event is to truly present yourself and your motivations to others while still being altruistic. #NetworkingTricks
http://aha.pub/StevenDavidElliot

50

When you present yourself as an honest, open, and transparent person who's open to listening and learning about others, there's a better chance they will like you. #NetworkingTricks http://aha.pub/StevenDavidElliot

Section III: Strategies for Being Successful at Physical Networking Events

51

People who do things without an ulterior motive are the ones who are most likely to be trusted. #NetworkingTricks
http://aha.pub/StevenDavidElliot

52

Something more important than setting goals for every networking event you attend is your "why." Why do you network?
http://aha.pub/StevenDavidElliot

53

Do you network because you want camaraderie and want to make friends with the people you meet? #WhatsYourWhy http://aha.pub/StevenDavidElliot

_____
_____
_____

54

Do you network because it's going to improve your ability to interact with your own clients or maybe you want to make more money? #WhatsYourWhy http://aha.pub/StevenDavidElliot

_____
_____
_____

Section III: Strategies for Being Successful at Physical Networking Events

55

Do you network because you have something to share with other people that you're passionate about and want to give voice to your passion? #WhatsYourWhy
http://aha.pub/StevenDavidElliot

56

When you've established your why and you're honest about it, you're closer to your goals, as it motivates you to keep striving for networking success.
http://aha.pub/StevenDavidElliot

57

If you take that leap and trust other people with your strengths, they're going to reward you by trusting you regardless of your warts and imperfections. #NetworkingTricks
http://aha.pub/StevenDavidElliot

Section IV: Your Keys to Success in Building a Good Referral Network

Share the AHA messages from this book socially by going to http://aha.pub/Mingle.

Section IV

Your Keys to Success in Building a Good Referral Network

Referrals can be a great contribution to your business's success. When you network, it's important to build a good referral network, which can help you and your business grow. The people you meet will refer you to their own sphere of influence if they know, like, and trust you.

When you help other people with their needs without expecting anything in return, people will see you as an authentic person. You'll be at the top of their mind—they'll say good things about you, refer people to you, and refer your business to the people they know.

58

Networking events are in demand because people want to meet as many people as they can to try and find the referral relationships they need. Are you attending enough networking events? http://aha.pub/StevenDavidElliot

59

The more you network and do good deeds for others, the more you are likely to receive a referral. #NetworkMore
http://aha.pub/StevenDavidElliot

60

Create #LocalNetworks because those are the people who can get to know you well, as they can connect with you physically.
http://aha.pub/StevenDavidElliot

Section IV: Your Keys to Success in Building a Good Referral Network

61

We do business with those we like and trust. We also recommend others whom we know, like, and trust. Do people know, like, and trust you? They should!
http://aha.pub/TEDtalk
http://aha.pub/NickCioffi

62

When people get to know and like you, there's a good chance they will trust you. When they trust you, they will refer business to you, recommend you, and potentially utilize your services.
http://aha.pub/StevenDavidElliot

63

If a person who's overly critical likes you, they'll be able to give you a very strong referral because people know how critical they are. http://aha.pub/StevenDavidElliot

64

The ripple effect of referral relationships starts when you're being authentic and helpful to others. http://aha.pub/NickCioffi

65

A valuable referral comes from your relationships with other people, the name that you build for yourself, and what you can do for others. Are you earning valuable referrals?
http://aha.pub/NickCioffi

_____
_____
_____

66

Thinking about other people's needs and trying to fulfill them is a great way to build trust and garner referrals. #Reciprocity
http://aha.pub/StevenDavidElliot

67

People will want to partner with you in your endeavors if they see that you have an interest in theirs. #Reciprocity
http://aha.pub/StevenDavidElliot

Section IV: Your Keys to Success in Building a Good Referral Network

68

A successful networker recognizes what other people's achievements are. When your network is a part of your conversation, it can lead to tremendous opportunities. http://aha.pub/StevenDavidElliot

_____
_____
_____

69

Physical networking is great because you can build #Relationships with people from different professions that not only help your business but also serve your clients. http://aha.pub/StevenDavidElliot

70

Your network should not just be filled with potential clients; it should be filled with people who can serve your clients and refer business to you. #CreateValuableConnections http://aha.pub/StevenDavidElliot

Section IV: Your Keys to Success in Building a Good Referral Network

71

Your network should include your colleagues who can help you understand how to serve your clients better.
#CreateValuableConnections
http://aha.pub/StevenDavidElliot

72

Your network should include people who can help establish you as an authority and make you a credible leader in your field.
#CreateValuableNetworks
http://aha.pub/StevenDavidElliot

73

Your network should be made up of people whom you can learn things from and people whom you can help.
#CreateValuableNetworks
http://aha.pub/StevenDavidElliot

74

If you are able to provide valuable referrals to the people in your network, you have legitimacy and credit in the referral bank.
http://aha.pub/StevenDavidElliot

Section IV: Your Keys to Success in Building a Good Referral Network

75

Your name will come to mind when your clients see that you have an excellent team and network that you share. #Leverage
http://aha.pub/StevenDavidElliot

76

If you have a large network that has interacted with you, they are the people who can speak to your legitimacy. Ask for testimonials when appropriate.
http://aha.pub/StevenDavidElliot

77

When you showcase your willingness to help others without expecting anything in return, it leads to the referral relationship you need for your business.
http://aha.pub/NickCioffi

78

When you help other people, they'll have good things to say about you when someone brings up your name. #WordOfMouth
http://aha.pub/StevenDavidElliot

Section IV: Your Keys to Success in Building a Good Referral Network

79

The benefit of helping other people is that they are the ones who will go out of their way to speak of the good deeds you are doing for the community. #Reciprocity
http://aha.pub/StevenDavidElliot

80

If you want introductions, the best way to get them is to make introductions. #Reciprocity
http://aha.pub/StevenDavidElliot

81

Your goal should be to take your new friends and introduce them to your old friends. By making mutual introductions, you're creating value.
http://aha.pub/StevenDavidElliot

82

When you become the connecting person between two people, that earns you their trust. http://aha.pub/StevenDavidElliot

83

A good networker is someone who goes out of their way to introduce other people so they may find value in each other. http://aha.pub/NickCioffi

84

The best networkers know how to introduce two people to one another who know absolutely nothing about each other and ensure that they have a meeting of the minds.
http://aha.pub/StevenDavidElliot

Section IV: Your Keys to Success in Building a Good Referral Network

85

Before making an introduction, it's sometimes good to speak to both parties to ensure interest and value in the introduction.
http://aha.pub/StevenDavidElliot

86

When you introduce two people to each other, you make an opportunity to join the conversation and follow up with them together as a group or individually.
http://aha.pub/StevenDavidElliot

87

You should help other people find their ideal clients by making appropriate introductions. When you've helped two people connect, you're at top of their mind for a period of time.
http://aha.pub/StevenDavidElliot

88

Make an introduction in a way that you're not aggrandizing the fact that you know people, but rather in a way that shows you want to help both parties.
http://aha.pub/StevenDavidElliot

89

By helping two other people without any expectations, you are turning a spotlight on yourself as a person who's altruistic and wants to help others.
http://aha.pub/StevenDavidElliot

90

You should be able to serve those in your network. If you aren't valuable to your network, your network won't be valuable to you. http://aha.pub/StevenDavidElliot

91

When people in your network connect with one another and have success, that success rolls over to you. http://aha.pub/StevenDavidElliot

Section V: Complement Your Physical Networking with Social Media

Share the AHA messages from this book socially by going to http://aha.pub/Mingle.

Section V

Complement Your Physical Networking with Social Media

Physically networking and meeting people in person at networking events has great value. If you want to increase the value of meeting people physically, you should accompany your physical networking with social networking. Complementing your physical networking with social media greatly cements the relationships you have with other people.

Section V: Complement Your Physical Networking with Social Media

92

The relationships you create and build with physical networking are even more valuable when you complement them with social media. http://aha.pub/NickCioffi

93

Networking has many forms. After meeting someone in person, they may see and pay attention to what you do with social media. #GrowYourRelationships http://aha.pub/NickCioffi

94

Physical networking is one-to-one marketing, whereas social media is one-to-many. Complement your physical networking with social media.
http://aha.pub/StevenDavidElliot

95

To be more successful in networking, you need to have an online presence to fuel the value and #Leverage what you're doing in person.
http://aha.pub/NickCioffi

Section V: Complement Your Physical Networking with Social Media

96

When you go to networking events, you can #Leverage your sphere of influence by connecting with them on social media. http://aha.pub/StevenDavidElliot

97

When people first meet you, they will often check out your online presence to verify who you are and learn more about you. #LeverageSocialMedia http://aha.pub/StevenDavidElliot

98

The Internet is the most powerful connector tool that the world has ever seen. It allows you to do things like be in 10 countries in the same day. Use it with your #PhysicalNetworking.
http://aha.pub/NickCioffi

Section V: Complement Your Physical Networking with Social Media

99

Complement face-to-face meetings by using #SocialMedia as a means to be reached or to reach others and follow up on people. http://aha.pub/NickCioffi

100

You can't get a ton of value out of your physical networking if you have no follow-up by phone, email, or social media. Have you followed up with your networks yet? http://aha.pub/NickCioffi

101

Social media is going to serve local people to you more frequently than international ones. They're the ones who can help you reach your goals. Don't take them for granted.
http://aha.pub/StevenDavidElliot

Section V: Complement Your Physical Networking with Social Media

102

Social media is a good tool to interact with people frequently—it can help cement the relationships you create with physical networking. Are you utilizing social media? http://aha.pub/StevenDavidElliot

_____
_____
_____

103

When you utilize social media in addition to your physical networking, you're able to create a mega sphere of networks. #LeverageSocialMedia
http://aha.pub/StevenDavidElliot

104

When you #Connect with people on social media after a networking event, you welcome them into your family and the relationship you have with them becomes a little more intimate.
http://aha.pub/StevenDavidElliot

Section V: Complement Your Physical Networking with Social Media

105

At networking events, everything centers around the in-person meeting. Finding people online and reconnecting with them digitally afterwards further cements the meeting.
http://aha.pub/NickCioffi

106

Congratulate people for their successes on social media and recognize colleagues who do similar things to you online. #ElevateYourStatus
http://aha.pub/StevenDavidElliot

107

In the past, we had limited ways to touch other people. Now, we can use social media to touch a lot of people from anywhere around the world. #MaximizeWithSocialMedia
http://aha.pub/StevenDavidElliot

Section V: Complement Your Physical Networking with Social Media

108

On Facebook, when you comment on what people say, you're joining their network and sphere of influence. #MaximizeWithSocialMedia
http://aha.pub/StevenDavidElliot

_____
_____
_____

109

If someone is celebrating something on Facebook or on LinkedIn that they are proud of, share in their happiness and their success. #Engage #MaximizeWithSocialMedia
http://aha.pub/NickCioffi

_____
_____
_____

110

If you want to be a more physical networker, utilize social media postings and #Engage with your clientele on Facebook and on LinkedIn. #MaximizeWithSocialMedia
http://aha.pub/StevenDavidElliot

111

On Facebook, a "love" doesn't cost you a penny more than a "like," but it's worth infinitely more to the person who's receiving it. #MaximizeWithSocialMedia
http://aha.pub/NickCioffi

Section V: Complement Your Physical Networking with Social Media

112

With social media, we can maintain a large network of people, since the majority of them have social media accounts for their business. #MaximizeWithSocialMedia
http://aha.pub/StevenDavidElliot

113

Maximize your ability to network successfully and garnish referral relationships and recommendations by utilizing #SocialMedia.
http://aha.pub/NickCioffi

114

There's no shame in letting people know what your interests are and what you do. Don't make it difficult for them to find you to do business with you. #BeAccessible http://aha.pub/NickCioffi

115

If you're going to be the leader and be seen as someone who can be trusted in business, your #SocialMediaPersona has to be neutral. http://aha.pub/StevenDavidElliot

116

Your social media reputation can impact your ability to monetize whatever career you have. Take care of it. http://aha.pub/NickCioffi

117

If you meet someone and have zero follow-up, it's as if your meeting didn't exist in the first place. #FollowUp http://aha.pub/StevenDavidElliot

118

Business people who incorporate both physical networking with social media get better results. Are you getting the results you want in business? http://aha.pub/NickCioffi

Section VI: Pitfalls of Networking to Avoid

Share the AHA messages from this book socially by going to
http://aha.pub/Mingle.

Section VI

Pitfalls of Networking to Avoid

When you go to networking events, you get to meet a lot of people—people who can be of value to you and your network, and people who can't. How do you handle the people you meet who can't be of value to you and your network if they ask for a referral? It's always important to think of your network first.

Networking can have its pitfalls, but it doesn't mean that those pitfalls overshadow the many great opportunities you can receive. Being aware of pitfalls can help you avoid them.

Section VI: Pitfalls of Networking to Avoid

119

When you're networking, you have to tread lightly to accommodate other people, even if you're the leader of the group. It's not about you; it's about the group as a whole.
http://aha.pub/StevenDavidElliot

120

Don't make introductions with
the expectation that you will
get introductions back
in return. #BeSelfless
http://aha.pub/StevenDavidElliot

121

Don't make inappropriate introductions
that can potentially waste someone in
your networking group's valuable time.
#PutYourGroupFirst
http://aha.pub/StevenDavidElliot

Section VI: Pitfalls of Networking to Avoid

122

What would you do when you're asked to recommend someone whom you don't know well? Be #Transparent and say why you don't feel comfortable making the recommendation.
http://aha.pub/StevenDavidElliot

123

If you're making inappropriate introductions, then you lose the trust in the people you're introducing. Are you making inappropriate introductions?
http://aha.pub/StevenDavidElliot

124

Just because someone says that they can offer you financial benefit does not mean that they're going to ultimately be beneficial to you and your network. #PutYourGroupFirst
http://aha.pub/StevenDavidElliot

125

If you make inappropriate introductions, people will neither take your introduction seriously nor value your ability as a matchmaker in business. #MakeAppropriateIntroductions
http://aha.pub/StevenDavidElliot

Section VI: Pitfalls of Networking to Avoid

126

If you say something controversial or offensive to other people on social media, that doesn't disappear. It stays out there in the Internet forever, and it could impact your ability to do business with other people. http://aha.pub/StevenDavidElliot

127

By not being careful with your social media presence, you are limiting your ability to be successful in gaining the respect and trust from others.
http://aha.pub/StevenDavidElliot

128

When you're a successful networker, you can no longer think of just yourself; think of your network and how bringing someone in who is inappropriate will negatively impact it. #PutYourGroupFirst
http://aha.pub/StevenDavidElliot

Section VII: Concluding Thoughts

Share the AHA messages from this book socially by going to http://aha.pub/Mingle.

Section VII

Concluding Thoughts

To be really successful in business, you need to have a group of people supporting you. What a better way to build your sphere of influence, your tribe, and your network than to host your own networking event.

Always remember that as individuals, we may fail, but as a group, we can succeed.

Section VII: Concluding Thoughts

129

As human beings, we do have a hunger and a human need to have interaction with people. Are you interacting enough?
http://aha.pub/NickCioffi

130

If you run a one-person business, one of your goals in networking should be to end your isolation. #Socialize
http://aha.pub/StevenDavidElliot

131

The human condition is naturally cooperative. When we isolate ourselves in our offices, we greatly stunt our ability to cooperate with one another. #Network
http://aha.pub/StevenDavidElliot

Section VII: Concluding Thoughts

132

With in-person networking, you are able to build trust with someone because you can see their true colors and their authenticity. #BuildRelationships http://aha.pub/NickCioffi

133

If you have an idea and want to put that idea in motion, you need a network to assist you. If you don't have that network, then start to build your sphere of influence today.
http://aha.pub/StevenDavidElliot

134

Networking events can help you refocus your goals and allow you to meet people who can help you reach those goals. How often do you go to networking events?
http://aha.pub/StevenDavidElliot

Section VII: Concluding Thoughts

135

How do you market to millennials or any group that you're not part of? Simple, interact with them to learn from them, and get to know how to meet their needs. http://aha.pub/StevenDavidElliot

_____
_____
_____

136

Networking can make you a better human by giving you the opportunity to put your words into action. #DoWhatYouSay
http://aha.pub/StevenDavidElliot

137

One key networking metric is being well known by the good deeds you do for others. Are you doing good things for others?
http://aha.pub/StevenDavidElliot

Section VII: Concluding Thoughts

138

Networking can produce big things for you and everyone else in your network. Are you being of value to your network?
http://aha.pub/StevenDavidElliot

139

People who create their own networks and build meaningful relationships tend to move in the direction towards #Success.
http://aha.pub/StevenDavidElliot

140

Want to be more successful in business? Create your own networking group and be the person others look up to.
http://aha.pub/StevenDavidElliot

_____
_____
_____

About the Authors

Steven David Elliot, CVO, created the Rockstar Connect program through years of experimentation and implementation. His networking events are legendary and are recognized as the "most successful and active in the world." He teaches that, through altruistic acts, you will be rewarded with material and spiritual abundance. As a REALTOR®, salesperson, connector, coach, and marketing expert, he has harnessed his ability to find options and solutions, limit them to the best, and help his clients select the outcomes to achieve their goals through active face-to-face networking.

Nick Cioffi is the co-founder and Chief Executive Officer for Rockstar Connect. He expanded Rockstar Connect from a one-off local event to an international company in hundreds of markets. His background in event creation and planning spans several years, and he is well known as a networking innovator. Through networking, he has grown his network into the thousands and established himself as a major influencer in the networking arena.

AHAthat makes it easy to share, author, and promote content. There are over 45,000 AHAmessages™ by thought leaders from around the world that you can share in seconds for free on Twitter, Facebook, LinkedIn, and Google+.

For those who want to author their own book, we have a 3-step, time-tested proven process that allows you to write your AHAbook™ of 140 digestible, bite-sized morsels and 5–8 blog posts. Once your content is on AHAthat, you have a customized link that you can use to have your fans/advocates share your content and help you grow your network.

- Start sharing: https://AHAthat.com
- Start authoring: https://AHAthat.com/Author

Please go directly to this book in AHAthat and share each AHAmessage socially at http://aha.pub/Mingle.